LOS ANGELES

History, People, Landmarks

HOLLYWOOD · DODGER STADIUM · CHINATOWN

PHILIP WOLNY

CURIOUS FOX BOOKS

© 2024 by Curious Fox Books™, an imprint of Fox Chapel Publishing Company, Inc., 903 Square Street, Mount Joy, PA 17552.

We Built This City: Los Angeles is a revision of *We Built This City: Los Angeles*, published in 2019 by Purple Toad Publishing, Inc. Reproduction of its contents is strictly prohibited without written permission from the rights holder.

Paperback ISBN 979-8-89094-048-3
Hardcover ISBN 979-8-89094-049-0

Library of Congress Control Number: 2023943822

To learn more about the other great books from Fox Chapel Publishing, or to find a retailer near you, call toll-free 800-457-9112 or visit us at *www.FoxChapelPublishing.com*.

We are always looking for talented authors. To submit an idea, please send a brief inquiry to acquisitions@foxchapelpublishing.com.

Fox Chapel Publishing makes every effort to use environmentally friendly paper for printing.

Printed in China

ABOUT THE AUTHOR: Philip Wolny was born in Poland, but has lived in the United States since the age of four. He is an author an editor, whose nonfiction titles for young-adult readers include books about U.S history, international politics, culture, religion, and many other topics. He lived in several neighborhoods of Los Angeles in the early to mid-2000s, including Los Feliz, Koreatown, and the Fairfax District, and remains a big booster of the city.

LOS ANGELES

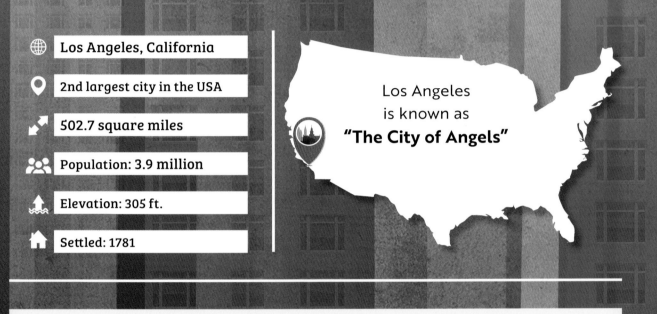

🌐 Los Angeles, California

📍 2nd largest city in the USA

↗ 502.7 square miles

👥 Population: 3.9 million

🌊 Elevation: 305 ft.

🏠 Settled: 1781

Los Angeles is known as **"The City of Angels"**

Los Angeles is a city that embodies the American dream to many—where palm-lined boulevards wind through flashy retail stores and golden beaches meet the Pacific Ocean. Los Angeles is not merely a city; it's a symbol of ambition, creativity, and limitless possibilities. From glamorous Hollywood to vibrant Chinatown, this city has diverse neighborhoods and world-famous landmarks. Explore the stories and places that create this captivating city. Welcome to Los Angeles!

CONTENTS

Top: Hikers take a break behind the Hollywood Sign. Bottom: The famous sign from below, as viewed from the neighborhood after which it was named.

Chapter One

A City Is Born

In the Hollywood Hills of Los Angeles, California, stands Mount Lee. Near the top of the 1,708-foot-high peak sits the world-famous Hollywood Sign. It has appeared in countless images, films, and television shows over the years, and has been the background for just as many smartphone selfies, taken by visitors from all over the world. If you stand behind the sign and look around, you can take in many of the sights that make "the City of Angels" one of the most famous and incredible metropolises in the world.

From the sign, you can see well-known neighborhoods such as the longtime entertainment capital of Hollywood, the soaring towers of Downtown Los Angeles, as well as the busy neighborhoods famous for immigrants' contributions, like Mexican-American Boyle Heights and Koreatown. On a clear day, you can see Venice and Santa Monica bordering the Pacific Ocean, and the mountain ranges that surround the city.

However, if you rewind about two hundred years, you would see a peaceful, empty landscape. Instead of city blocks going on for miles upon miles, skyscrapers, and freeways moving millions, there were thousands of acres of wetlands, forests, meadows, and other natural areas.

The Hollywood Sign has long been a symbol of the glitz and glamour of Los Angeles. But when you look at the huge, sprawling city from the top of the hill, ask yourself: "Who built these neighborhoods?

Narcisa Higuera, later known as Mrs. James V. Rosemeyre, was one of the last Tongva speakers.

Whose hands moved the billions of tons of materials to create the buildings, roads, parks, mansions, and other sights?"

The answer is everyday people, many of them from places like Mexico, China, Korea, Thailand, Japan, Europe, Armenia, Iran, and Russia. As much as any city, Los Angeles was built by immigrants, many of them poor, who had to fight for their rights as newcomers and citizens.

Before any other people lived in what is now Los Angeles, it was occupied by the indigenous people—that is, the people who originally settled there. They lived in the Los Angeles area for thousands of years before Europeans "discovered" North America.

The main group of people who lived in the greater Los Angeles area were the Tongva. They had neighbors, too, called the Tataviam. They lived in what is now northwest Los Angeles County and the southern part of Ventura County.

When grouped with some of their neighbors, the Tongva were estimated to number about 5,000 people as of 1770.[1] They built villages in the protected bay areas of the Pacific coast, and also alongside the streams and rivers in inland areas. Their land was some of the most fertile in the area. The Tongva were richer and more advanced than their neighbors, and influenced them in matters such as religion.

Imagine now that, instead of shining skyscrapers, parking lots, and apartment complexes, you are surrounded by the Los Angeles area of this earlier time. You could walk miles without seeing a soul.

If you stumbled on a Tongva village, you would encounter their domed homes, called *kish*. The Tongva placed wooden poles in the earth in a circle, and bent these to meet in the center. They would cover the

A Tongva *kish*, or home

frames with ferns or, more often, with reeds. The reeds were the leaves of the tule (TOO-lee) plant, which grew in the wetlands. They were also used to make boats and mats to sleep or sit on. Sometimes the Tongva would finish the roofs with mats of tule.

Their homes could fit up to sixty people, and three to four families would often live together. A typical village would have anywhere from fifty to two hundred people, according to early Spanish records.

The Tongva and their neighbors gathered acorns and plants, hunted animals and birds, and caught fish, sea lions, whales, and other sea creatures. They also made baskets, ceremonial artifacts, carvings, beads, and other artworks, many of which they used to trade with their neighbors. The area in which this small population lived—the Los Angeles area of the time—was more or less a wilderness compared to today.

The old sacred springs of the Tongva were long called the Serra Springs, after the Spanish missionary. They're now referred to as the Tongva Sacred Springs.

By 1829, Mission San Gabriel Arcángel was raising thousands of sheep and cattle. It also had one of the largest vineyards in Spanish California.

Junípero Serra is celebrated by some Americans and Spaniards for his missionary work. Many indigenous people, however, argue that under his leadership their people were killed, forced off their land, and made to give up their language and traditions.

The First Angelenos

The world the Tongva had known for hundreds of years would soon change in a big way. In the 1760s, Spanish colonizers arrived. They were led mainly by Roman Catholic missionaries—Spanish people who wanted to convert the Tongva people to their religion. Among the first and most famous structures they built was the Mission San Gabriel Arcángel. Founded in 1771 by Spaniards belonging to the Catholic religious order of the Franciscans, it was built in what is now modern-day Rosemead. This mission was moved to San Gabriel a few years later.

When Spanish colonizers first built settlements in 1769, they called the Tongva people the Gabrielinos (or Gabrieleños), because they were close to the San Gabriel mission. This went along with the Spanish tradition of naming native peoples after Spanish settlements. For example, the Spanish referred to the Tongva's northern neighbors, the Tataviam, as Fernandeños, because they lived near the Mission San Fernando Rey de España. This mission was founded in 1797 in the San Fernando Valley in what is now the suburb of Mission Hills.

The Spanish founded twenty-one missions throughout California in this era. A major leader in colonizing the region was Father Junípero Serra, a Franciscan priest. He started nine of these missions, including the one in San Gabriel.

Like other California tribes, the Tongva and their neighbors were forced to live on the new territories run by the Spanish missionaries. Those who were relocated were forced to give up their culture, language, religion, and traditions. Instead, they worked on raising

Native Americans plow fields near the Mission Basilica San Diego de Alcalá.

European crops and livestock. Though accounts vary, many historians agree that many of these people were treated little better than slaves for the newcomers. Those who refused or fought back were often punished or killed. Diseases brought by the Europeans likely killed the most people, however. Their population dwindled, and few signs of their original culture remain in Los Angeles.

The first eleven settler families—forty-four Spanish subjects from Mexico—formed a town, or pueblo, in 1781. Led by California Governor Felipe de Neve, it was called the Village of the Queen of the Angels ("El Pueblo de la Reina de los Angeles"). The name was later shortened to Los Angeles.

Pueblos were one of three kinds of settlements that the Spanish built in the New World. Pueblos were civilian towns, while missions were run by the church. The third type, presidios, or forts, were military bases of the Spanish Empire. For all intents and purposes, the Spanish residents of the Pueblo de Los Angeles could be considered among L.A.'s very first immigrants. Many of them worked on large areas of land

The pueblo of Los Angeles is shown circa 1869, with La Placita Church at the far left.

called ranchos (ranches), where they raised sheep and cattle for the wealthier landowners.

The newcomers, called pobladores (Spanish for "settlers"), were not simply of Spanish descent. Many were of mixed heritage, often partly African and partly Spanish, hailing from the Mexican states of Sinaloa and Sonora. Mestizos—those of mixed Spanish and indigenous Mexican heritage—would flock to the region in the coming decades.

Because of these changes, the landscape of L.A.'s previous thousand years or so began to change, too. Spanish-style colonial buildings took over the *kish*-dotted landscape of the Tongva and others. Churches, walled towns, and other structures like those in Spanish cities became a common sight.

In the nineteenth century, California and other parts of the West experienced even greater cultural change. The Spanish banned trading with most foreigners in the early 1800s, but they allowed ships from the new American nation. White Americans slowly but surely settled in the area, too.

By September 1821, Mexico gained independence from Spain, much like the U.S. had from Great Britain decades before. The area of California was now part of Mexico, and would remain so until the mid-century.

Perhaps the oldest house that remains standing in Los Angeles proper is the Ávila Adobe. Francisco Ávila was the son of Cornelio Ávila, one of the original soldiers who took control of the area. Francisco and his family arrived in the pueblo when he was two. He went on to become a rancher and one-time mayor of the pueblo. In 1818, he built a house on Olvera Street from adobe, a common building material of sun-dried clay brick. The house still stands in the historic district of Downtown Los Angeles.

The kitchen in the Ávila Adobe

Top: Many of the Chinese immigrants who came to the city worked on the Central Pacific Railroad. This was a massive undertaking of construction that completely reshaped the Sierra Nevada Mountains.
Bottom: Women walking through Chinatown, sometime around 1900.

Chapter Three

A City Expands

The middle of the nineteenth century was one of great change for both the United States and Mexico. From 1846 to 1848, the two nations faced off in the Mexican-American War. The U.S. victory gave it large sections of formerly Mexican land in the West, including California and several other states. A gold rush starting in 1848 brought as many as 300,000 settlers from other parts of the United States, mostly to the northern part of the state. The first discovery of gold in California was actually in Placerita Canyon, just north of Los Angeles. The news started a small local population boom. Many came for gold, of course, but others settled in the region to mine other metals, including silver and copper.

The town that began as *El Pueblo de Nuestra Señora la Reina de los Ángeles* expanded during this time, becoming Southern California's biggest town. While its population was only 141 around 1840, by 1850, that number had skyrocketed to 1,610.[1] Mexico's Congress decreed the pueblo a city in 1835. In 1850, two years after California was acquired by the United States in the treaty that ended the Mexican-American War, it was officially incorporated under the rules of the United States. Los Angeles could now collect taxes and elect its own officials.

In the 1850s, Chinese immigrants began to arrive in the city. Many of them found work with the Central Pacific Railroad, helping to construct the nation's first coast-to-coast, or transcontinental,

A stop on the Los Angeles & San Pedro Railroad. The transit link helped businesses in the region grow.

Chinese men walk in the city's Chinatown.

railway. The first L.A. neighborhood known as Chinatown sprang up near modern-day Downtown Los Angeles in the late 1800s.

As the population grew in the late nineteenth century, more jobs brought more people. Chinese and other workers did the heavy labor required for the 21-mile-long Los Angeles & San Pedro Railroad, built from 1868 to 1869. It connected the growing city with the port town of San Pedro. Older, larger Mexican ranches were divided into smaller farms and plantations. More immigrants, especially from

Mexico, tended to fill the jobs of picking crops and performing other types of tough, physical labor.

One of the most important political figures back then was Cristóbal Aguilar. He started as a city councilman, and then in 1866 was elected mayor. He set aside public land to create La Plaza Abaja, later known as Pershing Square, a park that remains a popular gathering place. While he was out of office for three months in 1867, Aguilar managed the city's water resources. One of his most important decisions was to refuse, or veto, the sale of the city's waterworks to a private company. Many city historians believe this veto was a main reason the city thrived so well at the time. Aguilar was the city's last Hispanic mayor until the 2005 election of Antonio Villaraigosa.

A modern park sits at the site of the original Pershing Square.

China Town

In 1870, around the time Aguilar won office a second time, the white population of Los Angeles outnumbered Hispanics and Native Americans for the first time. With the great wave of white settlers from other parts of the United States, non-white citizens were often outvoted in elections, and suffered from unjust and discriminatory laws.

Non-white workers often endured discrimination and violence when they tried to fight for their rights or demand better conditions. Chinese employees working on the First Transcontinental Railroad, for example, often had to work longer hours in more dangerous conditions, while making less than half the wages of white workers. When a tunnel explosion killed six workers, including five Chinese workers, it sparked a historic strike. Three thousand Chinese workers over thirty miles of track organized for equal wages and hours. The strike, unfortunately,

The original Los Angeles High School is shown in 1873 on Poundcake Hill, at the modern-day intersection of Temple Street and Fort Street (later known as Broadway).

was unsuccessful at first (the company owner cut off all food to the workers, forcing them to give in), but over the next few months, the company did raise wages for more experienced workers and the strike itself challenged stereotypes and inspired many.

Non-white citizens were also often forced by law or custom to live separately from whites, a practice known as segregation. Still, many of them created their own communities, where they preserved

A Chinese worker examines a section of damaged track. In 1867, Chinese immigrant laborers staged the largest strike of the era to fight for better pay and conditions, and to be treated equally compared to whites.

their languages and cultures, even as they fought for their full rights as Americans. In the meantime, white Americans soon became the majority not only in Los Angeles, but all across California.

One of the many groups who found ways to thrive and survive on their own terms were newly freed African Americans. After slavery was outlawed in the United States in 1865, a community of several hundred African Americans formed in the city.

Bridget "Biddy" Mason was a former slave who became a nurse, real estate investor, and landowner—one of the first black women to own land in the city. She and her son-in-law, Charles Owens, started a branch of the First African Methodist Episcopal (AME) Church. Using profits from land she owned near Downtown Los Angeles, Mason became one of the city's wealthiest and most well known citizens. She learned and spoke fluent Spanish, and she founded a black elementary school and a center to aid travelers.

Biddy Mason lived from 1818 to 1891. She had an amazing journey, from her birth into slavery, to being a pioneer in Colorado, and then becoming a rich investor in Los Angeles.

Top: Los Angeles annexed Wilmington and San Pedro as part of the port plan. Center: The city's first oil fields, shown here in the late 1890s, were near Toluca Street. Bottom: By 1913, the port had been dredged, allowing even larger ships to use it

Outward and Upward:
A World-Class City

The population of Los Angeles surpassed 100,000 in 1900. Many new developments helped it grow. The discovery of oil in and around Los Angeles and other parts of the state made California the nation's biggest petroleum producer. Oil jobs attracted even more people. Agriculture in the Los Angeles region also brought thousands of newcomers, including new immigrants from Mexico.

Many of them also helped lay more than 1,000 miles of track for the Pacific Electric Railway Company, founded in 1901. By 1920, this company was the world's largest electric railway. It connected distant parts of the region efficiently and cheaply. One of the most important destinations was San Pedro. It was already an important port town when Los Angeles annexed it, creating the new Port of Los Angeles. It became an even bigger center of commerce in the following decades.

As LA continued to develop, immigrants from around the globe traveled to the city looking for opportunity. A vibrant Korean community settled first in the Bunker Hill neighborhood and later moved to Olympic Boulevard, where Koreatown can still be explored. Little Tokyo is another historic spot in the city, one of a few places in the city where Japanese immigrants settled. Little Armenia and Little Moscow slowly grew up in Hollywood. Historic Filipinotown and Thai Town popped up. Neighborhoods like Boyle Heights became unique multicultural communities.

The Aqueduct was a huge and exciting project. Hundreds of people attended the opening celebration in 1913.

One of these new Americans who would change the face of Los Angeles was Irish immigrant William Muholland. He arrived in the city in 1877 at age 22. He was a civil engineer who would head the city's Bureau of Water Works and Supply. From 1907 to 1913, Mulholland led the building of the 233-mile Los Angeles Aqueduct, the biggest in the world then. Without this massive project and the water it provided, Los Angeles could not have grown as fast as it did.

Meanwhile, another group of immigrants would change Los Angeles in a wholly different way. Hollywood, about eight miles from Downtown, was originally a sleepy farming town. Instead of the buzz of paparazzi with cameras, imagine miles of sunny orange groves. A road between the two was equipped with a streetcar system in 1904—this would one day become Hollywood Boulevard. Hollywood residents voted to have Los Angeles annex their town because of the bigger city's new and advanced water supply.

The first movie studio in Hollywood, Nestor Studios, was started by Al Christie for David Horsley in 1911. Other famous immigrants who helped build the early film industry were Jews from Eastern and Central Europe. Among them were Polish-born Samuel Goldwyn (born Szmuel Gelbfisz), founder of Goldwyn Pictures, and Belarusian-born Louis B. Mayer (born Lazar Meir). They

Orange groves, like these in Southern California, were one of the main forms of land use in the area. Now, much of the region is highly developed.

Metro-Goldwyn-Mayer (MGM) Studios in 1916, This production company was located not in Hollywood but in Culver City, which is now a separate city surrounded by Los Angeles.

Modern Los Angeles is known for it's many complex highway systems.

co-founded Metro-Goldwyn-Mayer (MGM) Studios with Marcus Loew. Loew was the New York City–born son of Jewish immigrants from Austria and Germany. He would also start the Loews theater business.

By the mid-twentieth century, Los Angeles had expanded into a world-famous and world-class city. The freeways connected distant areas with Downtown and the beach areas. So did its streetcar system, which automobiles would soon replace. The first skyscrapers included the 32-story Los Angeles City Hall, built in 1928. Very tall buildings were not allowed by the city until voters decided to loosen the rules in 1957. The first new high-rise was the 40-story Union Bank building, completed in 1968. A race to build more skyscrapers occurred soon after, and the city's skyline was forever changed. Los Angeles was moving upward as well as outward. As of its 2017 completion, the

The Los Angeles Memorial Coliseum will soon host the Summer Olympics for a record third time.

Wilshire Grand Center was the tallest building in L.A. (and in California), at 1,100 feet.[1]

When a city is big enough, it can support major sports teams. Angelenos are proud of their teams, and their venues have become iconic landmarks. Los Angeles Memorial Coliseum was opened in 1923. It hosted the Summer Olympics twice, in 1932 and 1984, and

The Wilshire Grand Center shortly before it was finished.

The Capitol Records Building resembles a stack of vinyl records and is a Hollywood landmark.

will become the first stadium to have hosted the Summer Olympics three times in 2028. Until 1980, it was the home base for the Los Angeles Rams NFL franchise, and is still the home stadium for the University of Southern California's (USC) Trojans college football squad. Meanwhile, the Kia Forum in the Inglewood district was headquarters to both the Los Angeles Lakers basketball team and the Los Angeles Kings hockey team before they joined the Clippers basketball team at the Staples Center in Downtown (now known as the Crypto.com Arena), which opened in 1999. In 2024, the Clippers will open and move to the Intuit Dome, in cooperation with the city of Inglewood.

When baseball's Brooklyn Dodgers moved to Los Angeles, the city needed a stadium for them. Eventually, the Chavez Ravine area was selected as the site. "They literally moved mountains" to build the stadium, wrote Nathan Masters for KCET radio.[2] Workers moved eight million cubic yards of rock and earth to make room. Opened in 1962, the 56,000-seat home of the L.A. Dodgers remains the biggest professional baseball venue in the world.

Dodger Stadium, just north of Downtown Los Angeles, has become a landmark of the city, and a point of pride for its many baseball fans.

Top: Two musicians use a piano to test the acoustics on the grounds where L.A.'s famous outdoor music venue, the Hollywood Bowl, would be built. Center: The Hollywood Bowl in the modern era. Bottom: The venue in 1922.

Los Angeles into the Twenty-First Century

Well into the twenty-first century, Los Angeles has continued to grow and flourish. Long known for its highways, Los Angeles has invested millions in building up its transit system in the last few decades, especially its railways. In 1990, after many years without a true rail line, Los Angeles opened the Blue Line (now known as the A Line), connecting Downtown with Long Beach 22 miles away. Since then, five other lines have been built or relaunched to help connect the city, using about 115 miles of rail.[1] Many who lived there were happy, because it eased the terribly slow freeway and street traffic. Many more miles of rail will be built in the next decade, to prepare for when Los Angeles next hosts the Summer Olympics in 2028.

While directors shoot all over the United States, television and film are still one of L.A.'s most important industries. Every year, thousands of newcomers arrive to try to become stars, or to work in the many jobs that support the entertainment industry. Many more visit to take tours and fill audiences at places like CBS Television City in the Fairfax neighborhood, and at the combination theme park and production facility at Universal Studios. Most major studios offer in-depth tours where you can walk through sets and see their soundstages.

Music and other types of entertainment are also big industries. The Hollywood Bowl, for example, which opened in 1922, was named one of 2018's 10 best U.S. live music venues by *Rolling Stone* magazine.

The exterior of the J. Paul Getty Museum, also known as The Getty Center, showcases modern architectural details and art elements.

The Bowl is the home of the Hollywood Bowl Orchestra and the Los Angeles Philharmonic performs there throughout the summer. It also hosts hundreds of popular music concerts throughout the year.

As many as 47 million visitors flock to L.A. yearly, making tourism big business.[2] Besides its beaches, hiking, food, and nightlife, the arts and culture scenes have attracted painters, sculptors, and other artists to open studios. The Los Angeles County Museum of Art (LACMA), Museum of Contemporary Art, and the J. Paul Getty Museum are just a few of the dozens of famous art destinations.

The streets of the city provide their own history lessons. When exploring L.A., you will often encounter the names of famous residents

J. Paul Getty

who helped build the city, or had an impact on it. Some of the names are remembered in major streets and roads, or on landmark buildings and structures. The J. Paul Getty Museum was named after and financed by the fortune of the Getty family, whose oil business was once among the world's largest. William Mulholland has the famous Mulholland Drive named after him, as well as a dam and a middle school. Doheny Drive is named after another famous local oil tycoon, Edward L. Doheny. Wilshire

William Mulholland

Boulevard bears the name of Henry Gaylord Wilshire, who was not only a real estate developer, but also a socialist publisher and aspiring politician. This colorful character named the street for himself.

Social struggle and progressive politics are also reflected in L.A.'s street grid. In the 1960s and 1970s, Mexican-American labor activists Cesar Chavez and Dolores Huerta drew world attention by leading the United Farm Workers to protest unfair working conditions and

The city's lights sparkle like stars when viewed from the height of Mulholland Drive.

USC's Edward L. Doheny Memorial Library is one of many buildings and streets that pay honor to the city's major influencers.

pay. Huerta has had numerous schools named after her. Cesar Chavez Avenue runs a few miles through Downtown, and is one of several major streets named after Chavez throughout the world.

Los Angeles might look dramatically different in a couple of decades. There are plans to build new parkland—called "cap parks"—over several

Cesar Chavez

major sections of the city's freeways. One plan, called Park 101, would cover some of the 101 freeway extending through parts of Downtown. City planners and others also want to create new green space to run alongside the Los Angeles River. This famous concrete-lined waterway has been featured in dozens of movies, including the Terminator and Transformers franchises.

Although immigration and even birth rates are lower nowadays, Los Angeles's population hit the 4 million mark in 2017, according to

Hollywood (foreground), with Downtown Los Angeles in the back

the California Department of Finance.[3] Meanwhile, it was only in the twenty-first century that non-Hispanic whites actually became a minority in Los Angeles, a trend that will likely continue for some time. However it changes, Los Angeles will continue to be a cutting-edge, pioneering city for a long time to come.

Los Angeles is a city that embraces deep cultural history. In 2021, Jimi Castillo, the modern spiritual leader of the Tongva until his passing, prayed during the dedication ceremony of the Academy Museum of Motion Pictures.

Chronology

BCE	The Tongva settle in what will become California. Other nations eventually settle in the area as well, including the Chumash, Kitanemuk, Serrano, and Tataviam.
CE	
1771	The Mission San Gabriel Arcángel is established by Father Junípero Serra.
1781	El Pueblo de Nuestra Señora la Reina de los Ángeles del Río de Porciúncula is founded on a riverside, the first Spanish civilian settlement in Los Angeles.
1821	Mexico becomes independent from Spain. Its territories include California and other large parts of the West.
1848	The United States declares victory in the Mexican-American War. It takes over Los Angeles, making all Angelenos U.S. citizens. Gold is found in Placerita Canyon.
1865	Slavery is abolished. Several thousand newly freed African Americans move to Los Angeles.
1869	The Los Angeles & San Pedro is Southern California's first railway, running 21 miles to connect Downtown with San Pedro Bay.
1870	The white population of Los Angeles exceeds the population of Latinos and Native Americans for the first time.
1872	Biddy Mason establishes a branch of the First African Methodist Episcopal Church in Los Angeles.
1873	The city launches its first trolley system.
1880	The University of Southern California is founded.
1900	The population surpasses 100,000.
1913	The Los Angeles Aqueduct is built under the leadership of William Mulholland. It helps secure the city's water supply for many generations to come.
1915	Several large sections of the San Fernando Valley become part of Los Angeles proper.
1909	The city annexes Wilmington and San Pedro. Work begins on the Port of Los Angeles.
1920	Pacific Electric Railway Company becomes the largest electric railway in the country.
1932	Los Angeles hosts the Summer Olympics for the first time.
1939	Union Station, a major transit hub, is opened in Downtown Los Angeles.
1962	Dodger Stadium opens.
1973	Tom Bradley becomes mayor. He is only the second African American mayor in a major U.S. city.

Chronology

1980 The population passes more than 3 million people. Los Angeles passes Chicago, Illinois, to become the second most populous city in the nation, after New York City.

1984 Los Angeles again hosts the Olympic Games.

1990 The Los Angeles Metro Blue Line opens.

2005 Antonio Villaraigosa becomes the first Latino mayor of Los Angeles in 133 years.

2016 The population of Los Angeles hits 4 million for the first time.

2018 The Los Angeles Philharmonic celebrates one hundred years with its 2018–2019 season.

2021 SoFi Stadium opens in Inglewood

2022 Los Angeles Rams win the Super Bowl

2028 Los Angeles is scheduled to host the Olympic Games for the third time in its history.

Chapter Notes

CHAPTER 1. A CITY IS BORN

1. William McCawley, The First Angelinos: The Gabrielino Indians of Los Angeles (Banning, CA: Malki Museum Press; and Novato, CA: Ballena Press, 1996), p. 25.

CHAPTER 3. THE CITY EXPANDS

1. Los Angeles Almanac, http://www.laalmanac.com/index.php.

CHAPTER 4. OUTWARD AND UPWARD: A WORLD-CLASS CITY

1. Matthew Au, "A Brief History of Los Angeles' Tallest Buildings," KCET, February 11, 2014, https://www.kcet.org/shows/artbound/a-brief-history-of-los-angeles-tallest-buildings.

2. Nathan Masters, "They Moved Mountains to Build Dodger Stadium," KCET, October 11, 2013, https://www.kcet.org/shows/lost-la/they-moved-mountains-to-build-dodger-stadium.

CHAPTER 5. LOS ANGELES INTO THE TWENTY-FIRST CENTURY

1. L.A. Metro, "Facts at a Glance," https://www.metro.net/news/facts-glance.

2. Discoverlosangeles.com, "Los Angeles Welcomes a Record 47.3 Million Visitors in 2016." https://www.discoverlosangeles.com/travel/los-angeles-welcomed-a-record-473-million-visitors-in-2016

3. California Department of Finance, "New Demographic Report Shows California Population Nearing 40 Million Mark with Growth of 309,000 in 2017," May 1, 2018, https://htv-prod-media.s3.amazonaws.com/files/e-1-2018pressrelease-1525241227.pdf

Further Reading

Books

Bauer, Marion Dane, and C. B. Canga. *Celebrating California*. Boston: Houghton Mifflin Harcourt, 2013.

Erlic, Lily. *Los Angeles*. Calgary, AB: Weigl, 2017.

Orr, Tamra. *California*. New York: Children's Press/Scholastic, 2014.

Parhad, Elisa. *Los Angeles Is . . .* Petaluma, CA: Cameron Kids/Cameron + Company, 2018.

Tieck, Sarah. *California*. Minneapolis, MN: ABDO Publishing, 2013.

Works Consulted

Davis, Mike. *City of Quartz: Excavating the Future in Los Angeles*. Brooklyn, NY: Verso Books, 2006.

Heimann, Jim. *Los Angeles: Portrait of a City*. Los Angeles, CA: Taschen America, 2009.

McCawley, William. *The First Angelinos: The Gabrielino Indians of Los Angeles*. Banning, CA: Malki Museum Press; and Novato, CA: Ballena Press: 1996.

Stewart, Gail B. *Los Angeles (Great Cities of the USA)*. Vero Beach, FL: Rourke Enterprises, 1989.

On the Internet

City of Los Angeles
https://lacity.gov

County of Los Angeles
https://lacounty.gov

Discover Los Angeles
https://www.discoverlosangeles.com

Los Angeles Times
https://www.latimes.com

Glossary

adobe (uh-DOH-bee)—Clay made from natural materials, dried by the sun or other heat source, and made into bricks for building.

annex (AN-eks)—To claim or add another (usually) smaller territory to a larger one.

aqueduct (AK-wuh-dukt)—An above-ground channel built to move water from one place or another.

incorporate (in-KOR-por-ayt)—To give a town, city, or other community the power to elect its own officials.

indigenous (in-DIH-jih-nus)—Coming from, or native to, a place.

mestizo (meh-STEE-zoh)—A person in the New World who was of mixed European and indigenous background.

metropolis (meh-TRAH-pul-lis)—A large, well-populated city.

mission (MIH-shun)—An area claimed by representatives of the Catholic Church and used as a headquarters to convert native people to their religion.

paparazzi (pah-pah-RAHT-zee)—Photographers who follow and photograph celebrities in order to sell the photographs.

plantation (plan-TAY-shun)—A large farm on which crops are grown for profit.

pobladores (pah-blah-DOR-ays)—The Spanish term that means "settlers."

rancho (RON-choh)—The Spanish term for ranch, a large farm where the main business is raising cattle or other animals.

segregation (seh-greh-GAY-shun)—The practice of separating people according to their race or some other trait.

socialist (SOH-shuh-list)—A person who believes in a society in which there is no private property.

transcontinental (trans-kon-tih-NEN-tul)—Going from one side of a continent to the other, such as a railroad that connects the east and west coasts of North America.

tule (TOO-lee)—A plant with wide leaves that is native to wetland areas of California.

veto (VEE-toh)—The legal power to reject a decision or law.

Index